D1606171

No More Sorries

Step by Step guide into developing your greatness

By Monique Brown

Copyright © 2017 by Monique Brown

All rights reserved.

Published by Create space

Editor: Sheryl Corpus Photographer/Author Photo: Loren Alexander Cover Designer: Roger Peden

Library of Congress Cataloging-in-Publication Data

ISBN-13: 978-1973836681

ISBN-10: 1973836688

Printed in the United States of America

No parts of this book may be reproduced, stored in a retrieval system, or transmitted in any form or by any means, electronic, mechanical, photocopying, recording, or otherwise, without the prior written permission of the copyright owner. This book is sold subject to the condition that it shall not, by way of trade or otherwise, be lent, resold, hired out, or otherwise circulated without the publisher's prior consent in any form of binding or cover other than that in which it is published and without a similar condition including this condition being imposed on the subsequent purchaser. Under no circumstances may any part of this book be photocopied for resale.

Dear Mom,

You have taught me strength through your pain. When you tried having a normal life, your illness was eating away at you. You are my star, my everything. You have taught me the meaning of being true to myself. There are no days that I don't think of you. You are my true inspiration. For this, you are my strength and my encouragement. Because of you I stand!!! I miss you and I know you're with me each day, helping to inspire the world! You are my angel!! I love you!!! Rest in Paradise!! ~This is for you~

Your Daughter,

Monique Brown

Table of Content

What's inside of No More Sorries?

In No More Sorries, Monique Brown uncovers steps in which to implement in your daily life. This book is for your own personal growth. *"Each day we struggle, and those struggles become our strength"* – Monique Brown. She explains her story along each chapter and give out tools in creating your own greatness. No more Sorries explains that you should never allow people to get in your way, while reaching your goals. You will hear her motivation throughout each page, giving you inspiration, and realness. "To see change, we must be the change!"

Monique Brown

No More Sorries

To reach Mo Brown, visit her on:

Facebook.com/Mo Brown

Instagram.com/Mo_B_Motivation

Youtube.com/ Mo B Motivation

Email: Motivation729@gmail.com

Acknowledgements

I am dedicating this book to YOU! If you ever felt like no one was listening to you. When you are trying to put the puzzles pieces together, and just want to find you again. When you felt like your life is scattered and just want to find that peace and strength in your life to climb higher. This my friend is for YOU!!!

I also dedicate this to my family and friends who always supports me throughout life struggles and happiness. My two brothers Jason and Gene Brown, you two are amazing!! My grandparents Margaret (R.I.P) & bobby whom raised me. You two taught me greatly about this world, and everything that was taught to me, I will always remember.

This is for my Beautiful Partner/Best friend Brittany Brown through our ups and downs, each day we grow together. And I wouldn't trade that in the world. Caleb, I hope this inspires you to be the best version of yourself, be phenomenal.

This is dedicated to my Aunties, Aunt Sheila. You are like my second Mom, you have always supported me without hesitation, and seeing what you've been through, shows how much I admire you. I love you!! Aunt Sharon, T'laine, Shirley, Aunt Laura, and all my other Aunties. (Have a big family) My Uncles!!! Robert, Byron, Ramon, Derryck (RIP) there is a lot of you!!! All my Cousins!! All 5,000 of you!! Sabrina, Brian, Kitanda and the kids, Preshus (RIP), Franklin, Erica, E'zell, Nese, Ronesha, so many of you, it would take 10 years to write all of you, but you all know who you are!!

My amazing Nephew Gene, Auntie loves you!! My grandpa Gene and Deb, you guys always supported anything I do. Grandma Brown. All the Brown, Anderson, Campbell, Hawk, Mack, Williams, Wallace, and the Walker family. I love you all deeply!!!

I have more names, so if your name isn't on here, just know I got you on the next book. Picasso, me and you have been knowing each other for so many years. We've seen each other's highs and lows. I'm proud of you as an Artist, business men and a humble friend, I love you. Big Will I love that you strive for greatness through your positivity, and your willingness to push people to their own greatness. Charles Kellam aka the Philly cat, you are incredible comedian, author, mentor and friend. Thank you for helping me with words of wisdom, inspiration and anytime I needed you, you were always right there.

My bro Tri, thank you for always supporting me. My girls, AJ, Brishae, Malinda, Loren Ellen, P'nut,, you ladies are amazing!!! Always believed in my vision, loved and supported every step of the way, I love you!!! All my friends who were there through thick and thin!!!

My Pasadena and Long Beach Golds gym crew!!! My cardio dance class, hip hop!!! You guys gave me strength and smiles when anytime I taught class. You keep me going and I love you all so very much!!! Sam aka usher, you are amazing and talented man, thank you for always being here. Diego, you have always supported, gave me advice and always had my back when I needed fast music for my classes, and making sure my iPod was full of music. You're such an amazing light to me!! My girl Sherryl (Shay), who inspired me to start this book, who always stood by me through it all, and such a great Editor. Thank you for bringing this dream into a reality, I love you. Quandi "Q", WE DID IT!! You have inspired me to see more than just a layer, our talks and watching you grow has a true meaning. Eden for always believing in all my talents and being a mentor to me as well. Robb and Crystal Armstrong, you two inspire me to have a better relationship with my partner, you guys are full of life, love and talent, and you are family, thank you for everything, I love you both!!!

Carlos, you keep grinding in your growth, so proud!! Jessica Fram, you and I have known each other since H.I.U. You always stood by me, inspired me, listened to me, cared so much about me, your heart instills such brightness, and I am so happy to call you my family!! My guys who are amazing to me, Christopher and Kent. Thank you for always helping, supporting and believing in my dreams, I love you!!! Grace and Oasis family!! I love you all!!!!

This book is also for a special person who left to soon. You are my right and left. Every conversation we have had, we spoke about life, and how we treat it. When you smiled, you graced me with such light and love. This is for your inspiration, the hope and the dream. I will miss you always and for this I dedicate this to you Christopher "MITCHELL". Rest in Paradise....

My Story...

No more Sorries. Everyone's life becomes a story. Mines, came with adventure, death, heartache, worries, struggle, glory, joy, ambition, delegation, perseverance, compassion and love. At an early age, I have witnessed and underwent through many tribulations. I am one of 3 Children. My brothers' names are Jason (35 years old) and Gene (31 years old). Gene and I were the ones' who mostly watched my dad turn into an alcoholic and a drug dealer. My grandmother believed that he got my mom sick. My mother had Lupus. For the most part, she was in pain. She had multiple seizures. Due to my mother's illness, we lived with my Aunt Sheila for support. I watched my mother in pain. At 5 years old, I remember a lot of my nights would consist of my mother tapping my shoulders to tell me that she's going to have a seizure. I sympathized with my mother. I wanted to feel normalcy. I knew that my mother was attempting to have a "normal" life. Unfortunately, I saw the struggles she endured on a daily basis. At the age of 6, my mother passed. My grandmother raised us, along with our cousins. I would miss my mother and my grandmother would say "She's in heaven." My grandmother would tell me that she died with a broken heart. My mother endured the abuse that my father burdened her with. In addition, my father cheated on her. I knew that my mother had a heavy heart prior to her dying, but I was also relieved that she wasn't hurting anymore. I guess you can say, that I decipher people's hearts. At a young age, I knew that my mother's heart was filled with devastation. I felt sorry- I was sorry.

We weren't poor, but we had hand-me-downs. I was grateful for this. I was appreciative of my grandparents. They were strict, but gave us an abundance of love. My family were from New Orleans, so my grandmother can cook! We always had food on the table and never went hungry. I would get a whooping when I did something wrong, but would also receive positive praises for doing great things in my life. My family was all I had. I come from a family of strength, but also struggles. My grandmother died three times from different surgeries that was relayed from health issues like Diabetes.

I have learned so much from all the obstacles that I had to gone through. I was the type of person that would say "sorry" when the situation would be out of my hands, or doesn't even pertain to me. I would always tell myself, "Monique, stop being so damn sorry." My Aunt Sharon, who called me Nikki, would say, "Nikki, stop saying you're sorry, say you apologize." As I learned from life experiences, I finally concluded. Why would I apologize for things that can be changed? That simple, right? There are so many steps that one must take before understanding this concept.

I possess certain gifts and passion. My gift of music, dancing, and sports. I was around others that did not have the same talents or view of the world, as I did. Which, by the way was perfectly fine. Everyone have their own amazing talents. But, some individuals would use the fact, that maybe they did not have a talent as an excuse. But, I heart would feel for them. I was sorry. But, I realized, the more I felt sorry for them, the more they wanted me to keep being sorry. I guess the cliché, misery loves company, would fit in these situations. I accepted, understood, and dealt with this. I did this to myself. When I would mention my mom being deceased, I would typically hear, "Oh, I'm sorry to hear that." This replayed in my head over and over, until the words were part of my vocabulary and life. But, I realized that if I wanted to change, I have to be the change. Being, or saying, sorry should not be in my vocabulary. It should not dictate my life. I stopped feeling sorry for others because this is what enables others, including myself. We grow stronger with every journey we grow through. Getting stronger means not to apologize for the things that you cannot change. If you continue to apologize for the things that you can change, you will then not change and will not find the change that you seek.

As with any other person, my adult life also consisted of difficulties. I was in and out of relationships that I should not have been in. I helped others carry their own burdens. I felt used in these relationships because I allowed it to happen. I have had great relationships, don't get me wrong, I have had relationships that were positive. But when it came to matters of the heart with partners, I do not consider myself being "Pro." You see, I know what it feels like to be around alcoholism, abuse, and any other negative situation you can think of. I had my own baggage. I have had my share. I gave advice to those that were receptive. In the process, I completely ignored my own issues, and self-awareness, and that's when I started to feel sorry again. I understand that others are unable to be on the same journey that I am on. But, I am here to express how I overcame feeling sorry, versus pursuing. I don't mean to sound redundant, but if *I want change, then I have to be the change.*

I enrolled in a Christian University, majoring in business, with a minor in music. Studying in a Christian College gave me insight. This gave me the motivation to show others, especially myself, my capability. Meeting new people was a great experience as well. I've got to learn amazing cultures, and personalities besides my own. And being in a dormitory was a 24- hour fun zone! Which by the way, I rarely got sleep and studying done. Well, I guess that's the life of a young college student. But, as being a college student I had other responsibilities. I worked at In-n-out burgers, played college basketball and taught dancing to children (before I became a professional dancer). I created a dance group called "Seraphim" (translates to "Angels"). We would perform in half-time shows during Basketball season. And, in the midst of all these activities, I was also trying to become a recording artist, a R&B singer. The passion and drive that I have always possessed was one of my strong characteristic. That's how I thrive.

I have had experienced good times with people, but also challenging times. What made me change my thought of being sorry, was one instance, I had with a professor in my economics class. We had to write a Six-page term paper on our views of economics, and needed to turn in this paper before summer break. I put in a lot of hours to make it perfect. I even had some of my peers edit my paper. I remember him returning our papers, and when he gave me back my paper, he said, "See me after class." I was a bit nervous, because I didn't know why he wanted to see me. It bothered me. When I met with him, all I can remember from our conversation, was him saying, "Maybe going to college isn't right for you." My jaw dropped. Why would a professor, at a Christian college, discourage me? I felt so much hurt in my heart. I couldn't call my grandmother for comfort and support; she had already joined my mother in heaven. I was all alone. Now, I realized that feeling "sorry" was not an option anymore. I wanted to prove to myself that I can overcome this. During the summer break, I started writing a journal. I proof read the journal myself. I also worked in the summer, which made it tougher for me to do this; I did it though. When it was time to go back to school, I rewrote my term paper, and gave it to my economics professor. Three days later, he returned my term paper and said, "I'm sorry." He was speechless. He realized that it is important to believe and never doubt a persons' potential. He learned that day with me. I felt proud of myself because I proved him wrong. He doubted me, but I made the change for myself, not him. *If you want to see change, you have to be the change.*

Some of us want others to feel bad for us, but where does that take you? Are you attempting to get a sense of fulfillment? Are you trying to have a positive outlook of life? Maybe it's a hunch, but do you want others to feel sorry for you, because you want the attention? **STOP!!!** You need to understand that others do not reflect you, but can facilitate your actions (in a negative way). Because their energy may be negative, people will use your positive energy to find contentment.

Create your own journey and space. You will waste more time if you continue to feel sorry for situations/people you have no control over. Even though I didn't mention more of my struggles, every effort of me learning from all my hardships was worth it. I will outline the journey that will implement a better you, and better decisions that you will be able to make in your own journey. No longer sorry for uncontrollable forces. *Being sorry and apologetic are two different things.*

"The Journey of a thousand miles begins with a single step"

-Lao Tzu

Notes

Step 1

Stand Tall

In my old High School, I played Junior Varsity, and Varsity Basketball. We would go through our regular drill (dribbling the ball throughout the court) and practice running plays. It was fun, exhausting. By the end of the season, we were all extremely exhausted. My coach brought his good friend to watch us play. We did our routine drills and towards the end of our practice, we scrimmaged. I wanted to go home and rest. My coach's friend noticed that I had my head down during the drills. She walked towards me like she was a concerned drill sergeant. She said, "Hey!" I turned my head and walked to her like I was a child heading towards the principal's office. I replied, "Yes?" She stood there looking at me and paused for a good 5 minutes. Then she asked me, "Why are you putting your head down so much today?" I had no explanation, and all I can say was, "I'm tired." She smiled and said, "Never put your head down, stand tall and take pride!" I interpreted her words to be a reference towards me not appearing confident, but I was just tired and wanted to go home. During our last home game, I understood what she meant. My team needed me. I was a point guard and it was our last game. I was important and I had to deliver. I had worked an 8 hour shift the other night, plus studied for finals, I felt so fatigued. Playing basketball meant so much to me. I had to pull all the strength I had to play hard for the team. During the 4th quarter, my team had 40 points, and our rivals had 42 points. We had one minute on the clock. I started to put my head down, but I remembered what the coach's friend had said. I imagined her stern face and piercing eyes and remembered her saying, "Stand tall!" No matter what (win, lose, or draw), my team needed me, and I knew I needed ME. I needed ME to believe in MYSELF. As the crowd counted down, "5, 4, 3, 2, 1." the buzzer rang and our rivals shouted, "We did it."

I felt disappointed. I felt like I let my team down, as well as our school. As much as I wanted to place my hand over my head, I went to the locker room and spoke to my team. "We made it through!" As I looked around with tears in my teammates eyes, I felt a sense of pride.

Regardless of the outcome, we played amazing tonight! We've played the whole game with us kicking and fighting. This gave me understanding of the word "stand tall" and "take pride".

In our own life, we are faced with many challenges we may never want to face. We give up when things get too hard. We play the blame game, we opt-out. We often respond by wanting to put our heads down. You are stronger then that! Life's challenges create strength within ourselves. Remember that at times, we have no choice but to stand tall. Keep pushing and value your journey. There is always someone who is relying on you-YOU. *Stand Tall and Seize your way.*

Step 2

Hear the Truth

Have you ever had someone consistently complain about their own problems, to the point where they perceive everything in the world to be negative? It becomes redundant and annoying, when people gripe every day about the same issues. You start asking yourself, "Why? What's the purpose of whining all the time?" For some cases, people do this for attention and sympathy. By nature, we crave attention. This is apparent through social media (ie: Facebook, Instagram, Tweeter). In addition, people will post messages/pictures with hashtags, to get noticed more. It can be very confusing. The same negative people may say something positive in their hashtags (ie: #Doingme, #IAMSTRONG). They represent themselves as positive, but in all actuality, they are pessimistic and depressing.

So why do we use our energy on this? Know that we can change this type of behavior. Through my personal experiences, I've learn that society allows us to be free with our expression. Unfortunately, others are drawn to, and entertained by misfortunes and drama. Whether it be bad or good attention, it is still WANTED attention.

It is difficult for others to hear the truth. Can you tell a friend that they need to stop posting inappropriate, incriminating things? Can you ask them, "Is the number of likes you receive for these posts, more important than your dignity?" Why is it important to hear the truth? Because some may live carelessly through you. Our words can be strong and hurtful. We have all experienced someone who sought to bring us down, all because they felt low. *Misery loves company*, right? True friends, family, partner will tell you the truth. They will be honest and make you aware of the time wasted on your complaints.

Grab your life, and be happy. When we hear the truth, it becomes easier to include and exclude people in our journey. Remember, that it is vital to understand how amazing you are. We must stop listening to our friends, family, partner, make excuses for their behavior. The more we entertain other people's attention-seeking behaviors, the more we expend our energy by dealing with it. Use honesty and truth with love and compassion. If we don't, we repeat the same cycle. Grab your truth. ***Truth and Love guarantees positive results***

Notes

Step 3

Motivation

Looking for motivation can be extremely hard to implement into our life's. We want to be motivated to workout, find that new career, completing tasks on time, go back to school, etc. Sometimes our very own life eats our energy, whether it be family, jobs (that you may or may not like), relationships, so on and so forth. In my personal experiences, I allowed my own self to get in my way. I worked three (3) different jobs, which by the way I love. I was always excited to reach people and help motivate. I teach as a dance instructor at a gym. I'm like a trainer, and a trainer pushes and motivates. It is a rewarding job. I give my all to others, but lacked for myself. I was going through issues at home, dealing with deaths, having financial burdens, and developing health problems. I did not know where to begin or how to end them. These problems didn't arise at the same time. However, it felt like it. Every time one problem got fixed, another issue comes about. I slowly started lacking motivation for myself, I put too many eggs in my basket. I knew that I should be an example for those I encourage, but also remind myself that I am still human. Being not okay, was okay.

I personally believe that it is not our responsibilities that causes the lack of motivation but it's that we work harder for others than ourselves. So, when it's time to recharge, we have none to recharge with. After an exhausting day, and week, our brains don't shut off. Which gives us the illusion that our work is incomplete. We find the prompt ourselves to wake up, go to work, put on that happy smile, and take care of people. If we can use the same motivation to go and do activities we like (enroll in school, spending some you time, etc), then we are half-way there. Motivation is Motivation. But the things that motivate us the most (ie: bills, family), do not fully satisfies us, nor make us happy. Happiness is within. Where's a place you can go, that is only YOURS? Where no one knows about it. The place that can recharges you. Mine is the beach. I love the beach. I feel like it's my sanctuary. It fulfills my humbleness. I hear the voice of the ocean, and feel the sun shining on my skin. Every time I am at a point of exhaustion, I eagerly go to my place of peace to rid of the worries. I allow the waves to speak to me. And this is complete peacefulness. The most precious things on earth is at my disposal, and it's free!!! You can find a place like this- for YOURSELF.

We all deserve true happiness in life. It is vital to create for yourself. Take out the time to know your strength and all capacities. Speak special words into existence, this can give you a boost of inspiration. Every night and day, I take out five minutes to meditate and work on my breathing. When my eyes are closed, I focus on my center. I feel changed. I feel relief and possess the ability to start my day with love and positivity towards myself. This took a while for me to be comfortable with. I don't expect you to quickly be comfortable with your new place. But feel love, as you meditate. Just for clarification, I am not a meditation guru, but this helped me in my growth and journey. My Motivation is our God, earth, our life and passion. Motivation will always start and end with you.

"Optimism is faith that leads to achievement. Nothing can be done without hope and confidence".

–Helen Keller

Step 4

Make IT a PRIORITY!!

We've made choices that we aren't proud of. We hide our faces in our pillows so not to see ourselves grieve. When things get hard, we show our fear, our worries, our anxiety, (which by the way, does not help the situation). I had a great deal "trying" to figure out why I was in the same place in my life. There were several things that were easy for me to do, like teaching dance, working with kids, working out, creating some goals and accomplishing those goals. But why in some areas of my life did I feel stuck. I felt I was compelled to be there. I didn't know how to shake it off. But what I realize with my personal experiences, is that life has a pattern. Getting comfortable with the denial of growth. What I mean is that, there are times in each of our lives that opportunity knocks. A new position in our job/career, new relationship with someone you like, creating that new business, traveling etc. We decide to either become the doers, or the dont's. Simply put, the doers act and the don't doesn't.

Don't get me wrong, when we want something, we do everything in our power to get it. But my question is, no matter what the outcome of your goals are, why don't we take that effort and apply it towards what we want?! I've learned that I don't make this into a priority. It's super easy to make excuses about the things that are of no importance to us. We put it aside and pretend we don't have anything to do with it. I know it's easier to dismiss it. But it is much easier to take control, rather than let it control you. Start by realizing that you will not have everything completed. Make a list and this will be the beginning of your action. I usually, purchase a day planner. Each day, I write a few things that I can start and make sure I finish it by the end of the day. I give myself, three things to do each day, from Monday to Saturday. Sunday I rest and meditate. I also implement my yearly goals. I also have long-term goals. I have five to eight "must do's" and get them done that year. I make it my priority. Just like eating, drinking water, brushing your teeth is a priority to you, your goals are a priority too. In fact, it's a MUST. Little by little, when we reach our individual goals, we are a day closer to accomplishing our long-term goals. *Make it a Priority*

Notes

Step 5

Throwing away our worries

Years ago, I was approached by a woman who seemed extremely interested in me. Her smile seemed gazing, but I felt as if her attention was odd. She walked closer and I felt a little nervous because I didn't know her. It felt like eternity, with every footstep she took to get to me. Finally, she sat down beside me, and wanted to say something. I initiated the conversation by asking, "How are you?" With a smile, she replied, "Sad". I felt like she needed someone to talk to. I continue to ask her questions about why she felt sad. She explained that her mother died a month ago and she felt the need to approach me with this. I felt weird, but I believed it was a reason why we met. I mentioned that my mother passed when I was six. I completely understood and related to her. Her eyes were wide open, and she replied, "Wow, I can't believe it!" Her eyes started to water. I ask if I could pray for her. Her sadness seemed to subside. After a couple of hours of talking, she told me that she was worried about handling her mom's bills, her own bills, her job, etc. She had a lot of responsibilities on her shoulders and it was getting to her. I explained that life is like a curtained window. When we're ready to see the world, we open the curtain. When we want to be oblivious to the world, we leave it closed. When we first open the curtain, we may see cars driving by, people walking, and we hear people talking amongst each other, and all sort of other noises. We get nervous because we don't know how to cope with it. We feel it would be better if the curtain would just stay closed. But when this happens, our anxieties increase. Either way, reality is there. Better to face it, rather than to pretend it's not there.

How many times do we do this in our own life? When we struggle, we hide behind the curtains, thinking it would help our anxiety, pain, worries. In my life, I have had challenges that I had to cope with. It was very difficult. I knew that if I didn't control them, they will get the best of me. I started questioning about how to handle these issues. How do I overpower them? I open the curtains and open the window. I took deep breaths and chanted, "I'm okay". There is no magic pill for this. This will take time to do, but we must be consistent in creating progress in our lives. After being content, I tackle everything on my list, little by little. The major key in this is to be and stay consistent.

A good friend shared her story with me and informed me of what she did to overcome her concerns. She suggested to try it. So, I did and want to share this with you. Sit down in a quiet place, with a piece of paper in one hand and pen on the other. Think long and hard of all the doubts you have in your life. Create bullet points, or just write. There are several ways to do this activity, I am just explaining one. If you have friends you trust, gather them around and discuss these. Maybe meet at a beach where there are fire pits. Any place that would warrant a positive energy from you and everyone else. Serenity. Explain to your friends to write down their fears, dislikes, or whatever you choose to converse about. No one doesn't have to have knowledge of what everyone divulges in this group. This activity will help you not feel alone. Be honest, everyone has stressors. Set up a time, bring wood to burn, and gather your friends. Then, on a count of one to three, everyone throws their worries in the pit and bid "goodbyes." After this, don't look back. Breathe and say, "I'm okay," and really mean it.

Getting to the bottom of what makes us emotional, can be a task. It is never easy. Letting go of the very thing that keeps us from growing is a huge problem. It will affect our lives daily. I encourage you to search through your life and identify what's holding you back. Throw them away. It takes time. What's holding you? Whatever it is, toss it. It's time to take regulate your life. *Life has its own worries, don't make it your obligation*

Notes

Step 6

Energy Eaters

The title speaks for itself. We have those every day, hiding underneath whatever it wants to. Energy eaters maybe can be your close friend. Others can be family, and sometimes spouses. Throughout my life, I've had experiences where individuals either try, or eats up all the energy that took me so long to build. I mean, your finally at a comfortable place in your life, where you're happy. The birds are chirping the sun is shining. Before you know it, here comes the energy eaters. I got some news for you. Energy eaters were always there. Sometimes, we at first don't see them. We might have not noticed them even the second time around. We start learning how to accept ourselves, and don't give energy eaters our drive. However, when we are sometimes set free, and on cloud nine, they will show up and we finally see them. The reason why the "energy eaters" didn't show up the first time, or even the second, is because you didn't have anything to give. It's like people knowing you have no car, no one comes to you. Suddenly, you have one and everyone now wants to be a part of it, they want to ride it and take up the gas.

Energy eaters, need to be fed. They will prey on you until they have depleted you and go on to the next person. But, what's great about our strength, is that we can make a choice. Make choices as to who and what we want to give our energy to. When someone constantly tries to complain about their lives to you and don't want to change it, they become a parasite. A Parasite that keeps hanging onto you. This creates conflicts, disagreements, arguments, and other unwanted situations. Thus, making you feel lethargic. This type of problem often happens when we are improving our lives. Whether it be completing school to graduate, obtaining a new career, possessing a new car, having vacations, etc., can make an "energy eater" hungry. Some people call them "haters", I'll call them energy eaters.

I had a dear friend, who called me every day to vent. She would explain detail by detail, about situation after situation. It got exhausting. One day, she called me while I was studying. I did not feel like being bothered. I explained that I'm busy and needed to call her back. Her reaction felt like someone put hot lava on my hands. It was to the point that every other sentence was, "You've made me feel." Like I had something to do with whatever she was dealing with. She made me feel guilty about not talking to her. I realized that this person did not care about my well-being, only hers. The nights I stood up and listen to this person nag and nag, gave me more of a reason to keep myself away. Not only was she draining me, but I felt like she wanted me to be a victim of her problems. All she wanted from me was to hear her gripes. She didn't care that I had things and needed to do.

We all have a good heart, and want to support someone by listening to all their issues. They will often talk to a person that they trust, but will have any regards to that person. It can become tiresome. This can affect your personally. When dealing with that type of person, it is best to walk away. When they call, let them leave a message. Not everything deserves your attention. Be cautious of who you talk to and practice personal space. It starts with you. Use your energy on the things that's important to you, and that will help you grow and persevere. It's crucial to eliminate people who refuse to grow. Learn and develop yourself. Stay away from people who are always negative and refuse to change.

Surround yourself with like-minded people and move forward. Be aware of the energy eaters. Practice thinking of serenity and keep that in your head. ***Energy shouldn't be wasted, it should be practiced.***

Notes

Step7

Pretender's Prescription

Warning** Pretender's may cause depression, anxiety, laziness, lack of self-worth, inability to understand others, attention seeking, drama, and a lack of ambition.

Have you ever experience these type of side effects? Have you ever had someone act as a friend to you, but to only mislead you and make your life a living hell because their life isn't where they want it to be? He/she sees you striving to accomplish and complete your goals. He/she spots the happiness and memories you're developing for yourself. Your friend may want you to think he/she is happy for your accomplishments. Some of our friends might be genuine, but there are some who we need to be aware of. We keep busy, so we have tunnel vision. These so called "friend" have their own agendas. They sit, plot, and wait until we fall. We will however, will sometimes fall in our lives. But it is very important to have those friends that can catch us when we are falling.

I have amazing friends and family who supports me, but I've had a few snakes in my grass. Sometimes past relationships can hold you up. The crazy thing about it, we don't even know it. We don't realize it until things get worse. I had an Ex, who pretended that she supported me. This individual would only "show" support because others did. And when I would teach a class, I would return home only to get cursed out. She did this because of all the insecurities she had. I repeatedly told her that there was nothing to be insecure about. Every day, I would try so many times to convince her of this. Nothing seemed to work. I started feeling like the Jack-in-the box. Do you remember that? You would have to turn the handle counter clock wise for it to work and hear the music. And after a certain amount of turns, Jack would pop out. I felt like the Jack in that relationship, and the one who was turning the handle was my Ex. You can imagine how depressing that was. There were times after work, I dreaded going home. But the crazy thing about this whole situation, was that this was not my battle to fight. I made it my battle when I kept "getting in the ring." When I was unhappy, she seemed to love it. When I was happy, she seemed like she wasn't. Eventually I realize that I had to remove myself away from that situation and move out. I absolutely did! I finally got my peace and strength back. Sometimes in our lives, we must hit rock bottom and feel vulnerable to see a change. I remember my Aunt Sheila would always tell me, "Never think that you're stuck". Every day I take that to heart.

Sometimes we feel like we should cater to people to feel special. Ignore our feelings, and emotions. What I've realized is that people who are always negative, loves misery. They love to drag you with them. The Steps that you have read so far explains that YOU actually control YOU. Take back your environment, your space. Separate yourself from individuals that use your energy in a non-healthy way. If their trying to stop you from your goals, then it's time to remove yourself. You must want it, and know that your life and health is too important than someone else's drama.

We cannot control others, but we can dictate what we want and what we allow in our life. I can't blame my Ex because it was me who allowed that negative flow in my life. We must be accountable for own actions, our own responsibilities. We will always have someone who may be that snake in the grass, but it's up us to keep our grass cut short. Observe, feel what your spirit is speaking, and listen to it. Mind you, not everyone will be that snake, but not everyone is deserving to be in your presence. So, watch the company you do keep.

Stay focus on your ambition, the things that power you. Give light to it. Build, and embrace like-minded people in your journey, and be honest with them. Most importantly, be true to yourself. This will help you separate the good apples from the bad ones. The only way you will see those "Pretender Prescription," is if you feel the effects. ***Be your own natural Medicine***

Notes

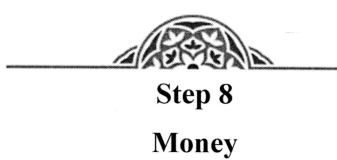

Step 8

Money

Think of *money* as a metaphor for life. Each day, our world consists of one thing, valuing money. Money has a way of changing people's behaviors too. It can also create loads of stress, anxiety, and even depression. Some of us may know what it feels like. It is a cycle. We work, get paid, pay bills, take care of our children, and tend the house. Then, we repeat. You'll leave the bank with a certain amount in your hand, but only to be left with nothing. It's like you work so hard each day and feel like you only get less of what you've worked. I mean, at least it feels that way. Why the metaphor? Because I feel that money really represents our lives. Money is our energy, power, motivation. Believe it or not, people in our lives can deplete it. They create insufficient funds, and overdrafts.

We are all responsible. We allow the people we love and care about, spend our "money." They leave us with nothing. Think about a situation in your life when you lost all control, when you felt powerless. When did you feel lonely, vulnerable, and ashamed? We are, at times, are fortunate to have run into people who mean well, and do well. This does help us control our situation. It gets extremely difficult when we get taken advantage of by others that do not care for us. We feel the need to make them understand why it is important to take care of our money. But it's your responsibility! We would give our vulnerability to unworthy people. We paint this big picture and assume that things will be right. In the past, I gave certain people my time, and space, only to feel empty at the end of the day. I gave them my money, and all I was left with were receipts. I took back the dignity that I had given them. I gave myself another chance. You want to start checking your balances, watch what you spend, and create your budget. Be careful who you give your time, energy, and your love to. Your money is earned and valuable. I can only imagine how you feel right now, what to do and how to act on it. We can give. It is easier to give, than to receive, in most of us. Learn how to invest in your life. This is about our personal growth. Go with your first instinct, we all have it. Practice listening to yourself. Make your money grow for you. Stay away from individuals that takes, without returning anything back. I am not suggesting, to forget those that genuinely care and love you. But to simply look at your circle. Learn to identify whether your circle is supportive and value your time, or whether they are wasting it. *Second guessing yourself only proves that your first thought was right.*

Recapping Steps:

- Be accountable

- Take Control

- Choose your circle wisely

- Bring people in your life that can ADD value

- Follow your instincts

Step 9
Changing our way of thinking through actions

Changing the direction of how we think is a big step of understanding who YOU are. There are many ways to approach this kind of thinking. Just like words are powerful, so is thinking. You can only imagine what your journey is going to be like, or where it will lead you. It's all how we think. Our mind controls our body. Our mind tells our body to move, eat, sleep and such. It can be difficult to implement change when your mind is elsewhere. But it's not that our mind can't change. It's due to not changing our actions. It's like we have a battle against our brain and our body. For example, let's just say, you've been wanting to work out. In your mind you're mentally ready, but your body doesn't want to move. I believe that when we change our actions, our mind changes, and vice versa. Let's use the same scenario, our body is ready to work out, but our mind doesn't want to. We are in conflict about wanting to alter ourselves but don't know where to begin. Frustration comes about. The reason being, this is so time consuming. We get overwhelmed when we put so much on ourselves. We feel like giving up. We often feel like not starting.

We have all heard the saying, "If we change the way we think, then we will change." I agree, I even use this idea myself. But we must realize that there is more than one way to understand this. Each day, we are faced with different tasks. Some may be big, and some may be small. Some may be difficult and some easy. But regardless of the task we face, our actions should speak louder than words. To complete your task, our actions must be aligned with what needs to be completed. Our mentality must be towards the actions. How can we align them both?! You should write your patterns. What have you done in the past? How did you react when facing something traumatic? What did you do when you experienced being hurt? Did you show your depression by being in bed all day? Or, did you go out and kept yourself busy in a positive way? These are the things we need to be mindful of. From my experience, I've noticed that when I felt inspired, I have the energy to carry out what I need to, to gain the result I wanted. When we need money, we go to work. Acquiring money is the goal. The thought of working hard, is the battle. Earn it! It's not that our thought process is screwed up, it's because we can be pushed by the things we know we need to do, instead of what we want to do. This is why it can be difficult to change the way we think through our actions.

EXERCISE:

List five things that motivates you, and list five more of which you would like to complete (goals, etc.) You can say a bucket list. Now, number each item. One being the highest and five being the lowest. For example, here is my list:

Motivating (Now)	**Goals to Complete (Future)**
1. Job	1. Publishing my first Manuscript
2. Teaching Classes/Working out	2. Running a Marathon
3. Inspiring/Motivating people	3. Writing a second book

That was just an example. I realized that procrastination also contributes to one not finishing the tasks needed to reach the goals. Our goals collect dust, like the book you were always wanting to finish. What are something that motivates and inspires you? And what happens next? Do you act on it? Do you stand still? "Do you ignore it?" Have one goal at a time and accomplish them. After you finish, cross that out and go to the next goal. Give yourself five goals only, or however many you think you are capable of doing!! The reason why I ask for only five, is because we get quickly overwhelm and want to give up without even starting. Write down actual goals that you think you need to accomplish. Do things for your well-being and what you love (ie: traveling, starting a business, getting a better job, writing your first book, better relationship, etc.) After this step, put it in the envelope. Seal it and put it somewhere safe. Open it by the end of the year. And look back to see if you reached your goal. If you only accomplish some, take the remaining goals and rewrite it in your list, for your next year's goals. Add more goals if you know you are capable of finishing. Your anxiety can lessen if you do this exercise. It's also a way to promise yourself to act on your needs. Trust yourself enough to make the move. This is all your responsibility. On the way to the top, don't forget that you will have struggles, they make you stronger. Change your actions, and your mind will change. Be that belief, and your growth will come through your actions. ***Become YOUR Difference.***

Notes

Step 10
Your day start and ends
with you

There is always a start and a finish. For example, when you and some of your closest friends watch a basketball game, there is a beginning and an end. There's a 1st quarter and after the 4th, you have the ending score. We don't realize that our lives are very similar. You go to work at 9am and get off at 5pm. During the time you are occupied, what is it that you do, to finish your day. Did you have a smile? What I have experienced and notice, is that we don't end our day off positive. In fact, we bring our job to our homes. We force ourselves to be conscious without living. We do not take value. We must realize our day can be so amazing, if we could only feel that way. What's stopping you though? The answer is YOU! We assume, that in order for us to have a terrific day, others must make it terrific for us. Wrong! You control your destiny, your drive.

Our beginning and end, is our birth and death. What we do in between are up to us and how we decipher. The people that you choose to be around, or the relationship you choose to have, starts and ends with you. It's up to you to have a great life. But you must accept the struggles. Be okay with what you do during your lifetime and grab that phenomenal finish, instead of that crappy finish. We have the mind power to create a fantastic finish. Start by creating unity with yourself. To create this unity, we must diminish our negative thoughts. For example, when you wake up and get ready for work, instead of feeling depressed, and hitting snooze every eight minutes, wake up and tell yourself that today will be a great day. Speak this through repetitions. Use positive motivational words in your statements and thinking. If you love music, play music without words, such as Jazz, or some sort of soothing music. Perhaps, watch motivational videos. These few examples, will help guide you. Everyone is different. Use and practice positivity in your language. Once you speak, so shall it be. ***Your own words can make or break you.***

Notes

Step 11

Love Them from a Distance

Now, this step can be hard to do. And this really takes practice. But, you can do it! We help and support people throughout our lives. We have a heart of gold. We give so much of ourselves away. And sometimes people just desire too much from us. We even deal with people who constantly nags about redundant things in their life. We choose to stay in that unenthusiastic mood. And somehow it keeps you from going farther in your own life. We are too busy with other people and the drama they carry. The more we respond by supporting their habits, the less we accomplish for ourselves.

You do not have to be around people, if you don't want to. That's the beauty of having our own mind. You elect to be around anyone you choose. But why is it so hard to love them from a distance? Because, people can be manipulative. They will use the simplest words. Vision this. You're at the grocery store, just only to purchase a few items. You do not plan on doing anything else. You get a text from a friend. This is how conversation went:

Friend: "Where are you?"

You: "At the grocery store."

Friend: "Can you pick me up?"

You: "Where are you?"

Friend: "An hour away from you. My boyfriend has my car and I do not have money for Uber."

Now, remember, you have picked your friend up from different places, multiple times. He/she somehow convinces you to pick him/her up because of his/her manipulation. He/she then texts you, "If you can't, I'll understand." Would she? He/she chooses you, because you have helped him/her so many other times. He/she are the ones always complaining to you. What is so different now? You basically know this person's life. Every time, you start a new adventure, he/she calls you to complain about her life. Again, this drains you from the inside and out. You do not want to feel bad, so you listen to her sob story. So, why does this friend choose not to change? Is it because he/she doesn't want to? Is it because he/she has no desire to do so? She would rather complain all day and night. You ask, how can I love someone from a distance? Well, I am glad you ask. You learn about yourself. Learn about what you can tolerate and what you can't. You will get to a point in your life, where you have nothing else to give to people, or better yet, to yourself. After hitting rock bottom, you will gradually start to move in another direction subconsciously. You then will realize how important you are. You will learn to say, "No," to things and situations in your life. Learn to be okay with the word NO. When your friend calls and does the same thing, you will simply reply, "NO, I am busy". Then, you have that time to focus on you more, and not others. You do not have to remove yourself completely from their lives, but get them to understand, that you care about you more.

It is always hard to say No to people you care so deeply about, but understand if they felt the same way you felt, it would be a completely different ball game. Do more for yourself, and learn to say," No." Add it to your vocabulary. This is not to tell you, that you should not be there for your friends, family, spouse, etc. It's simply telling you, that you cannot put all your eggs in their basket. We must make ways, figure it out, and act. Allow them to figure their situations out, while still loving and caring for them from afar. Focus on you, and allow them to fix and take care of their own problems. Love them from a distance. ***Best way to see growth, is to distance yourself from negative situations.***

Notes

Step 12

Determination

We experience unstable moments. We try to understand our purpose of those rocky moments. How we understand, you ask? Through battles and battles of willpower. When we go through something, we are determined to get out of it. We have bumps and brushes during our journey in life, just to reach for that determination. We question our abilities and strengths. But life will not give you struggles, if you weren't ready. When we experience pain, and helplessness, believe it or not we gain strength from it. When someone doubt us, we are determined to prove them wrong. And what I mean by "them", is the people that are around us. Our friends and family. We have ambition to create something in life, and the first person that may doubt, is not only people around us, it's who we look at in the mirror every morning, yep, it's us! You see, it's not about finding determination through people, we need to find it through ourselves.

Every experience we go through will be different. And at times, we must dig deep to gather that strength, keep focus and move forward. You are chosen to experience these struggles, because you can handle them.

Sometimes, people can motivate us to push harder, and it might help, but relying on others can be a bad habit. The reason, is that we are doing it for the wrong purpose. Don't get me wrong, it is always great to find something or someone to help start our motivation, but it should be us to finish, because we need to! When we look around, our life gradually starts making sense. We realize, we are supposed to be where we supposed to be. Two years ago, I was diagnosed with Grave Disease. Of course, I was afraid, this diagnosed was new for me. I had to do some research, and asked myself why was I diagnosed with Grave Disease? After researching, it gave me a new perspective. And it made me dig deeper. I used this as DETERMINATION. Having Grave Disease, I've experienced fatigue, hand tremors, brain fog, heat intolerance, palpitation, vision problems, insomnia, nervousness, some muscle weakness, and weight gain and loss. But I was still DETERMINE!!! I had to challenge myself, push myself. And if I never experienced determination, this book would not be written.

No more of looking at our situations and being upset about it. We have been put on this earth to do great things, and yes, we will struggle, this will help us to get to our determination. We have perseverance. We are special and unique. We embody power. There is no one like us. We are individually made perfect. Anything we face, we will defeat. I am Determine, you are Determine and We are Determine. So, grab a whole of your determination and let it lead you to greatness!!! **Winning isn't about numbers, it's your drive that creates Wins!!!**

Step 13

Self-Forgiveness

It's not your fault! The worse thing that we do is blame ourselves. It takes so long for us to forgive us. We count how many wrong things we have done, the imperfection. We don't look at the strength that we have develop, during those hard times. We take on the blame, because we feel compelled to. It is always great to forgive others, but the best feeling is when we forgive our own self. In fact, this can be a lot easier to forgive other's, then ourselves. But, it all depends on the situation.

Let me say this, **it is okay, to not be okay**. Not everything we deal with, will be perfect. And no, there will be people who will never understand you. But, we must learn that it is not our obligation to get them to understand us. Each of us, live in different journeys of our life's, and along the way, will be choices that we make. Some choices we make, will be bad choices, other choices, we make will be good ones. And in that time, we will often learn from the bad to get to the good.

In my personal experiences, I had to deal with my own imperfections. Some people looked at me as perfect, when I did not see that for myself. People seen what I didn't. Because I was too busy looking at all my own flaws, and being disappointed at myself. Blaming myself, and yes, doubting my ability. But I knew I had to change what I was feeling, so, I went to the beach one day, and was just glaring at the sun setting. Suddenly, tears just flow through my eyes. I could not stop them from flowing. All the pain that I put myself through, because I did not know how to forgive myself. I closed my eyes, breathed in with my nose and out with my mouth, and I spoke life back into my life. I forgave myself for the first time. And it felt amazing! I use empowerment words like:

"I am amazing"

"I am so proud of me"

"I am so beautiful"

"I forgive me"

"I am Phenomenal"

"I am full of greatness and talents"

It was not people who hurt me, or even the people that had passed away, that I've lost. It was me, not allowing myself to grow. We can get in our own way. And I've got in my own way. When I started to practice words of motivation for myself, I no longer had no chip on my shoulders. We must realize that we all have a past. Past is something that you cannot go back to. But, will prepare us for our future. We are HUMAN! Realize it! Forgiving ourselves will be the greatest accomplishment. Forgiving others like I have mentioned earlier, is also a must. It will help you to move on with your life, and prepare yourself for blessings ahead. Time does not stop. We are the only ones that have that control button in our hands. We create our own destiny. Find your peace. Know that you are special, and uniquely made perfect. We are created to be awesome in our life, and that's including going through struggles. Love yourself more, bring life by using positive words about you! We all have something to share to the world, and we cannot share them, if we cannot forgive ourselves. Forgive yourself, and let unwanted things go, that will be the only way to find your peace. Because, *YOU ARE PEACE!*

Step 14

No More Sorries

Throw away all your pain, animosity, hurt, discouragement, and self-doubt. Begin to show your inner strength. And Realize that you are worth more than your past. No more excuses for wasting time with people who have or had negative intentions. You will persevere! Be proud of your steps. Do not apologize for your growth. For this will help shape you to be the best version of yourself. What we go through in life, only explains how magnificent our future will be. Carry on the torch of love, admiration, and appreciation. Worry less and do more!

No more being sorry for the things you can change!! Take control and responsibilities for your life. Try and keep trying, do and keep doing, love and keep loving, smile and keep smiling. Build and keep building. No more Sorries! No more excuses! No more pity!

Have Pride! Grab your happiness, it's yours! And take positive risks! This is about you, and your growth as a human. This is about taking what is yours. Stop apologizing for other people's mistakes, and for your mistakes. Accept the fact, that we may not always get it right the first time, or even the second. But, once we keep being determined, there will be no need to be sorry!!

It's time to begin a new chapter with your life. Begin by loving you more, believing in yourself, and being able to see how awesome YOU are! Stay honest with your feelings and face those fears. Be patience with you. Never look back! And for that, you are **NOT SORRY!!!**

YOU ARE NOT SORRY FOR BEING
WHO YOU ARE.

Notes

Epilogue: From Me to You....

This book was written for all of us. This teaches us to face our fears despite the naysayers. To believe in what we have, and what we can give ourselves. Being aware of our changes, and being okay with them. I've gone through many changes in my life. Seen some horrible things, as well as amazing things. Perseverance is a great attribute to develop. Which I know that YOU all have!!!

Life isn't about being perfect, life is about experiencing your moments. It's all about pushing. And not apologizing for your growth. This book "No More Sorries", is from me to you. Whatever life hands, you keep going!! When you feel like giving up, don't!! As a child, I looked at how my mother reacted to her pain. I've seen her cry. I've seen her look at me with such strength. But I also seen her at her weakest points, and so many visits to the hospital. Throughout all of what I have seen, I never seen her **GIVE UP!!**

So, when life have you, and you feel like it's over for you, it's not! Your struggles will be your strength, and it becomes your testimony. Be proud of you right now! You took this step because you want to see change, and that you value YOU!! So, with that being said....

Congratulations!!!!

So proud of you

Testimonies

"I started participating in Mo's "Cardio Hip Hop" class about 3 years ago. I must say that she is an awesome instructor, as well as, a motivational person. She encourages us in every class as she sweats the pounds off of us. Her classes are always packed and we fight to be on the front row. She stays current with her music and her routines. She would even dance for us as a treat when we worked out really hard. I think the thing that everyone likes about Monique is that she genuinely cares about people. We're not just her students in her class, we are her friends."

-Dr. Damita Johnson

Thank you!

drdamita2@gmail.com

"Monique is a very encouraging person. She's the type of person who wants to see everyone win in life. Creating a healthy lifestyle starts with your mental health. Monique strives to inspire others to have a healthy mind and body with her words of encouragement. Life is full of obstacles and Monique teaches others to look at things that you may be struggling with as a opportunity for growth. For example, I personally have struggled with my weight all my life. Monique took time out of her busy schedule to assist me with a diet plan that worked for me. Her training is designed based on the individual. Nothing cookie cutter about it. I look forward to what the future holds for her."

-Sabrina Williams

"I took Mo's class about 6 years ago. My goal was to drop in and tryout Cardio Dance. I had no plans of taking more classes after that. After taking the first class, I became hooked and I am still taking her class six years later. Mo is a great Cardio teacher. She uses the latest dance tunes in her fast up beat classes. While using great choreography, she challenges us with moves that all levels could learn because she breaks it down. What makes her unique is that she really loves her students. She is not like some teachers who come to class to just teach. Furthermore, Mo is a great as a teacher and she inspired me to teach."

-Stacey Porter

"I am writing to you this to let you know about my beautiful Cardio Dance Instructor and friend Monique Brown. She has been an inspiration to me and her great energy and words of wisdom convinced me to become a Zumba instructor at the age of 45. I currently reside in Long Beach and I am so glad I moved here or I would have never met such an ambitious, special and unique person. I have never taken a Cardio Dance class like MO's. She is a great leader that has instilled confidence and encouragement in me. I struggle everyday with my weight and personal issues and it is so comforting to know that I have an unlimited amount of praise and support from her. She pours out her love to her students, Cardio class members, she received her Bachelor's Degree and now is about to publish a book. I am blessed to know such an incredible woman and I look forward to doing her Cardio Dance classes every week. Mo believes in me and her positive quotes lift me up and have impacted me on days that were essential to my well-being. I love Monique Brown and she will forever be my friend and Cardio Dance Instructor. She is a brilliant, creative and a loving human being that is humble and has a lot of humility. I did not get to where I am alone and Mo definitely has been a great influence in my life!"

-Michelle Castillo

"Life isn't about finding yourself. Life is about creating yourself."

-George Bernard Shaw

"Don't forget to love yourself."

-Soren Kierkegaard

"Strength and growth come only through continuous effort and struggle."

-Napoleon Hill

"Perseverance is falling 19 times and succeeding the 20th"

-Julie Andrews

Thank you for all your support, be inspired!!!

-Monique Brown